The Titanic

Other titles in the *American Disasters* series:

The Challenger Disaster
Tragic Space Flight
ISBN 0-7660-1222-0

The Exxon Valdez
Tragic Oil Spill
ISBN 0-7660-1058-9

Fire in Oakland, California
Billion-Dollar Blaze
ISBN 0-7660-1220-4

Hurricane Andrew
Nature's Rage
ISBN 0-7660-1057-0

The L.A. Riots
Rage in the City of Angels
ISBN 0-7660-1219-0

The Mighty Midwest Flood
Raging Rivers
ISBN 0-7660-1221-2

Mount St. Helens Volcano
Violent Eruption
ISBN 0-7660-1552-1

The Oklahoma City Bombing
Terror in the Heartland
ISBN 0-7660-1061-9

Plains Outbreak Tornadoes
Killer Twisters
ISBN 0-7660-1059-7

San Francisco Earthquake, 1989
Death and Destruction
ISBN 0-7660-1060-0

The Siege at Waco
Deadly Inferno
ISBN 0-7660-1218-2

TWA Flight 800
Explosion in Midair
ISBN 0-7660-1217-4

The World Trade Center Bombing
Terror in the Towers
ISBN 0-7660-1056-2

The Titanic

Disaster at Sea

Michael D. Cole

Enslow Publishers, Inc.

40 Industrial Road
Box 398
Berkeley Heights, NJ 07922
USA

PO Box 38
Aldershot
Hants GU12 6BP
UK

http://www.enslow.com

Library of Congress Cataloging-in-Publication Data

Cole, Michael D.
The Titanic : disaster at sea / Michael D. Cole.
p. cm. — (American disasters)
Includes bibliographical references and index.
ISBN 0-7660-1557-2
1. Titanic (Steamship)—Juvenile literature.
2. Shipwrecks—North Atlantic Ocean—Juvenile literature.
[1. Titanic (Steamship) 2. Shipwrecks.] I. Title. II. Series.
G530.T6 C66 2001
910'.91634—dc21

00-009423

Printed in the United States of America

10 9 8 7 6 5 4 3 2 1

To Our Readers:
All Internet Addresses in this book were active and appropriate when we went to press. Any comments or suggestions can be sent by e-mail to Comments@enslow.com or to the address on the back cover.

Illustration Credits: AP/Wide World Photos, pp. 6, 36, 38, 40, 41; Six Titanic Paintings Cards, John Batchelor, Dover Publications, Inc., pp. 1, 18, 25; Story of the "Titanic" Cards, Frank O. Braynard, Dover Publications, Inc., pp. 8, 9, 13, 14, 17, 20, 22, 27, 28, 31, 34.

Cover Illustration: Six Titanic Paintings Cards, John Batchelor, Dover Publications, Inc.

Contents

Pictured is an antique poster advertising the White Star Line of passenger ships. White Star's *Titanic* was "the largest steamer in the world," and thought to be unsinkable.

CHAPTER 1

Unsinkable

It was 12:15 A.M. on April 15, 1912. Harold Cottam was operating the wireless communication system aboard the steamer ship *Carpathia.* Cottam was almost done with his shift when a series of Morse code messages started to come through. He quickly sat down to decode them.

"Require immediate assistance . . . Come at once . . . We have struck an iceberg . . . sinking." The message was followed by the location of the ship and the letters CQD, which meant "Come, Quick, Danger." The message also included the letters MGY.[1]

Cottam was shocked. The letters MGY were the code symbols for the *Titanic.*

Newspapers around the world had been filled with stories about the *Titanic* as it prepared for its maiden voyage across the Atlantic Ocean, from England to New York. The *Titanic* was the largest ocean liner ever built. Its engineering and design were state-of-the-art. Builders believed the mighty ship was virtually unsinkable.

The *Titanic* is shown here at its first launching on May 31, 1911. It would sink during its maiden voyage less than a year later.

The *Titanic* had departed from England five days earlier on April 10, 1912. After stops in France and Ireland to pick up more passengers, the *Titanic* steamed out to sea. More than 2,000 passengers and crew were aboard.

Cottam quickly informed his captain of the message he had just heard. Fifty-eight miles away, the *Titanic* was sinking.

Aboard the doomed ship, little more than half an hour had passed since lookout Frederick Fleet had spotted a dark mass in the distance.

"Iceberg right ahead," Fleet had quickly warned the officers on the bridge. But the giant ship had not turned in time, and scraped the side of the iceberg. In a matter of seconds, the ship's fate had been sealed. The iceberg had opened the *Titanic*'s hull. Water flooded into the forward compartments.[2]

The terrible news then spread through the crew and passengers. The *Titanic* had struck an iceberg and was going down. Stewards moved quickly across the ship's many decks. Passengers were told to get to the lifeboat deck and put on their lifejackets. For the next two hours,

Workers try to fit the starboard propeller shaft into its position on the *Titanic*'s stern. The propeller was 23½ feet in diameter.

a tragic drama would unfold upon the decks of the *Titanic*. The ill-fated ship and its passengers were about to slip into history.

Even before its maiden voyage, the *Titanic* had become a kind of symbol. Its great size and luxury represented the best that could be produced with that era's wealth and know-how. People of all classes, from the very rich to the very poor, were aboard the ship that night. The loss of so many lives aboard the *Titanic* made the ship's sinking a great tragedy.

The *Titanic* began as a triumph of the human spirit. It represented the human desire to build things bigger and better. Its end would be a reminder that nothing on the sea is unsinkable, and that nothing in the world is certain.

CHAPTER 2

The Biggest and Finest

In the early twentieth century, traveling was very different than it is today. There was no air travel for regular passengers. Airplanes had just been invented. Travel by ship was sometimes rough. Crossing the Atlantic sometimes meant week-long voyages aboard ships. Conditions were usually not comfortable or relaxing.

The British owners and builders of the White Star Line of ships had been trying to change the style of sea travel since 1870. In that year, the White Star Line launched its first ship, the *Oceanic*. It had many features that made travel more comfortable for passengers. The company built five other ocean liners between 1899 and 1907. Each one set a new record for size.

By 1909, the technology existed not only to build the ships larger, but to fit them with engines that were faster and more reliable. The White Star Line set out to build a new fleet of liners of extreme luxury to appeal to the world's wealthiest travelers. J. Bruce Ismay, manager of the White Star Line, wanted to build three ships— the *Olympic*, the *Titanic*, and the *Gigantic*. The *Olympic* was built first and successfully launched in October 1910. But the *Titanic* was to be even bigger, and more luxurious.[1]

Construction on the hull of the *Titanic* began in March 1909 at the shipyard of the Harland and Wolff shipbuilding firm in Belfast, Ireland. The *Titanic*'s hull was 882 feet long, nearly the length of three football fields. The design included nine decks, making the ship as tall as an eleven-story building. It was driven by three giant steam engines which were powered by twenty-nine boilers. Each boiler was fifteen feet high and weighed more than one hundred tons. When completed, the ship contained 25,000 tons of steel, held together by more than 3 million rivets.[2]

An important part of the ship's design was the sixteen separate watertight compartments in the hull. If a collision were to rip a hole anywhere in the hull, the compartments would then be sealed off by giant iron doors. Sealing off the area that was taking on water would keep the water from spreading through the rest of the ship. Even if three of the sixteen compartments became completely filled with water, the ship would still stay afloat. No one ever imagined a collision would occur that could damage three compartments.

"I cannot conceive of any vital disaster happening to this vessel," said Captain Edward Smith after taking command of the *Titanic*. "Modern shipbuilding has gone beyond that." After a long and successful career at sea, Captain Smith had been scheduled to take the *Titanic*'s maiden voyage as his last command before retiring. Captain Smith would carry out his duties to the end, but he would not retire.[3]

The *Titanic*'s giant hull was launched on May 31, 1911. The rest of its structure, including the many cabins, restaurants, saloons, lounges, and even a gym, were completed later as the ship remained secured at dry dock. A dry dock is a structure that holds a ship in place while it is completed or repaired. No expense was spared in the decoration of the first- and second-class passengers'

Lord William James Pirrie (left), chairman of the Harland and Wolff shipbuilding firm, and J. Bruce Ismay (right), chairman of the White Star Line, inspect the *Olympic* before its launching at Belfast in 1910.

The *Olympic* (left) and the *Titanic* (right) at Belfast.

suites. Their furnishings included more than thirty different kinds of chairs, fifty varieties of tables, oak beds, brass beds, and electric heaters. Some of the rooms had oak paneling and a fireplace.

When the *Titanic* was completed in April 1912, it performed beautifully in sea trials. Then builders signed papers that turned ownership of the *Titanic* over to the White Star Line. Publicity describing the ship's size and design generated a great deal of public interest. A 1911 edition of the magazine *Shipbuilder* described how the ship's special watertight doors would save the *Titanic* in case of collision at sea.

"The Captain may, by simply moving an electric

switch, instantly close the doors throughout and make the vessel practically unsinkable," one writer claimed.[4] Many similar claims that the huge ship was unsinkable appeared in other magazines and newspapers.

The ship's maiden voyage would depart from Southampton, England, on April 10, 1912. The passenger list for this voyage included some of the richest and most famous people in the world. This created even more public interest in the ship.[5]

Wealthy American industrialist Benjamin Guggenheim would be aboard. Isidor Straus, founder of the world-famous *Macy's* department store in New York City, was traveling with his wife. John Jacob Astor IV, the wealthy great-grandson of the famous American fur trader, would also be on board. Margaret Brown, the wife of Denver millionaire James J. Brown, would be traveling without her husband aboard the *Titanic*. Known to her friends as "Molly," Brown's actions during the ship's sinking would become legendary.

More than half of the ship's passengers were traveling in third class. Passage aboard this part of the ship was inexpensive. The third-class areas had none of the luxuries or comforts enjoyed by passengers on the upper decks. Many of these third-class passengers were immigrants from Europe. They were making their way across the Atlantic Ocean to start a new life in the United States.[6]

At noon on April 10, 1912, with great fanfare, the *Titanic* pulled away from the dock at Southampton, England. The British crew numbered 892. They included the men in the engineering rooms, the stewards, cooks, waiters, and storekeepers, and the officers on the bridge. On this first voyage of the giant new ship, the White Star Line's president, J. Bruce Ismay, was aboard to observe. Thomas Andrews, the chief designer of the *Titanic*, was also aboard to see how the ship performed, both at sea and at providing comfort and amusement to its passengers.

The *Titanic* crossed the English Channel, and stopped twice to take on additional passengers. First it stopped at Cherbourg, France, and then at Queenstown, Ireland. When the ship steamed away from Ireland on the afternoon of April 11, the official count was 1,316 passengers and 892 crew, for a total of 2,208 aboard. Passengers enjoyed themselves for the next three days and nights aboard the lavish ship.

The *Titanic* was equipped with a wireless communication system, an early form of radio. Radio voice communication had not yet been developed, so wireless operators sent and received messages tapped out in Morse code. On April 14, the *Titanic*'s wireless operators began receiving a number of iceberg warnings from other ships. Despite the warnings, Captain Smith gave orders for an increase in speed. He pushed the ship to 22½ knots (about 23 miles per hour). Other ice warnings continued to come in.[7]

At 11:40 P.M., lookouts Frederick Fleet and Reginald Lee were struggling to stay warm in the ship's crow's nest. The crow's nest is a lookout tower near the front of a ship. There two sailors could scan the sea ahead of the ship to

Above is the bedroom of a first-class suite (Cabin B 59) aboard the *Titanic*. Below is the ship's gymnasium, which included a swimming pool and a squash court.

make sure the way was clear. Mist moving across the water was making their job more difficult.

Suddenly Fleet spotted a dark mass in the distance directly ahead of the ship. He quickly rang the alarm bell three times. Then he grabbed the telephone to give the duty officer on the bridge an urgent report.

"Are you there?" Fleet asked.

"Yes," the officer responded. "What do you see?"

"Iceberg right ahead."[8]

On the evening of April 14, 1912, the captain of the *Titanic* ordered an increase in speed despite repeated iceberg warnings.

CHAPTER 3

The Impossible Happens

The officers on the *Titanic*'s bridge reacted quickly.

"Iceberg right ahead!" Junior Officer James Moody repeated to First Officer William Murdoch.

"Hard-a-starboard," Murdoch quickly ordered. The quartermaster, the sailor at the ship's wheel, spun the wheel hard to the right until it would turn no more.[1]

Seconds later, Murdoch ordered the engine room to stop and reverse the engines. This was done to slow the ship's movement toward the iceberg. Preparing for the worst, Murdoch also hit the switch that closed the watertight doors to the hull compartments. As the officers on the bridge and the men in the engine room waited, the *Titanic* slowly turned.[2]

But the ship had been going too fast. Its speed made it impossible to stop the giant vessel before it reached the iceberg. The ship was also not turning fast enough. The order to stop and reverse engines made the ship's steering more sluggish. If the engines had only been slowed,

The grand staircase of the *Titanic* descended from the boat deck into the A Deck first-class entrance foyer.

rather than reversed, the ship would have actually turned faster.

In the crow's nest, Fleet and Lee braced themselves for a collision. Several large chunks of ice fell onto the ship's decks as the *Titanic* brushed along the iceberg and drifted onward to a stop minutes later. Crew members on the deck were relieved. The ship's bow, or forward section, appeared to have missed the iceberg.[3]

But many of those elsewhere in the ship knew better. Passengers and crew in different parts of the ship either felt a shock or heard a scraping noise. The *Titanic* had struck a part of the iceberg below the waterline. Engineers

Fred Barrett and James Hesketh were in the number six boiler room near the front of the ship. Suddenly the right-side wall of their room crashed open and water gushed in. Hesketh escaped the flood of seawater in the room just before the huge, watertight door slammed shut, sealing the room off from the rest of the ship. Barrett used the emergency escape ladder. The two men were safe for the moment. But the damage to the *Titanic* was more serious than a single hole in a single compartment.

A hard, jagged piece of ice had cut into the lower part of the bow as the ship passed by. It had left a line of holes and crumpled steel along a 300-foot stretch of the hull. Cold sea water was now rushing into the number one hold, number two hold, number three hold, number six boiler room, and number five boiler room.

"What have we struck?" asked Captain Smith when he stepped onto the bridge.

"An iceberg, sir," First Officer Murdoch replied. He explained that he had turned the ship, cut the engines, and closed the watertight doors.[4]

The collision had lasted only ten seconds, but the wound the iceberg had inflicted was fatal. The water flowing into the forward portion of the ship below decks could not be stopped.

The *Titanic*'s chief designer, Thomas Andrews, was unaware that anything had happened until he heard a knock at his cabin door. A crewman told him to report quickly to the bridge. When Andrews arrived, Captain Smith informed him of the collision. He asked Andrews to

Lord Pirrie and Captain Edward J. Smith (right). Captain Smith had planned to retire after the *Titanic* completed its maiden voyage.

accompany him on an inspection of the damage. Their inspection of the shocking scene below decks at the ship's forward area lasted less than ten minutes. The compartments were flooding, and Andrews slowly realized that the watertight doors were not going to stop the inflow of water. The men returned to the bridge, where their discussion was brief.

The iceberg had cut a gash so long that it was filling the front five compartments with water. The watertight doors in boiler rooms six and five went only as high as the ship's E deck. As the weight of the water pulled the front of the ship down, the water from the number six boiler room would flow into number five. This would pull the ship even lower, causing the water to flow into the number four boiler room. It would then flow into number three, then number two, and so on.

Andrews's conclusion was grim. There was nothing

they could do to change the ship's fate. It was already certain. The *Titanic* was doomed.

"How long have we?" Captain Smith asked.

"An hour and a half," Andrews replied. "Possibly two. Not much longer."

Wasting no time, Captain Smith immediately mobilized his crew. "Uncover the boats," he ordered.[5]

The ship's general alarm was never sounded. The alarm might have caused a panic among the passengers that would have made abandoning the ship more difficult. Instead, officers were sent through the ship to inform the rest of the crew of the collision. Stewards walked through the decks, telling passengers, many of whom were in bed, to dress and put on lifejackets. When the ship's position was calculated, Captain Smith delivered it to John Phillips and Harold Bride, the ship's wireless operators.

"We've struck an iceberg," Smith told them. "Send the call for assistance." Phillips and Bride went to work at once.[6]

Details about the ship's damage were not communicated to every crew member. Some stewards were unable to tell passengers exactly what had happened, and many passengers could not believe there was any real danger. The result was confusion about the urgency to get to the lifeboats.

At 12:10 A.M., passenger Elizabeth Shutes saw a ship's officer and asked if there was any danger.

"No," the officer responded, trying to avoid the spread of panic. But as he went further down the corridor, Shutes overheard him say to another crewman, "I think we can keep the water out a bit longer."[7]

Margaret "Molly" Brown heard the news that they were to get ready to abandon ship. After traveling in Egypt, she had a collection of Egyptian relics in her cabin. Just before leaving, Molly grabbed one of the pieces. It was a small figurine. She took it with her for good luck.

Ruth Becker was only twelve years old. She was traveling with her mother and younger brother and sister. A steward told them to get ready to leave quickly.

"Do we have time to dress?" Ruth's mother asked.

"You have time for nothing," the steward replied. "Put on your lifejackets and come up to the boat deck." Ruth helped her mother dress her baby brother and sister. They were in such a hurry they forgot to put on their lifejackets.[8]

At that moment, few if any passengers knew the grim truth about the lifeboats. There were not nearly enough. The sixteen wooden lifeboats and the four collapsible boats on board could keep a total of 1,178 people afloat. But there were 2,208 aboard the *Titanic*. That meant that 1,030 people would be without lifeboats. Strangely, the law did not require the ship to carry enough boats for everyone.

Anyone who tried to escape the ship by jumping into the water with or without a lifejacket would freeze in a short time in the icy waters of the Atlantic. Unless another ship came, those without a lifeboat would not survive.

Despite the fact that the crew had never conducted a

An hour after the *Titanic*'s fatal collision with an iceberg, women and children began to be loaded into the ship's lifeboats.

lifeboat drill on the *Titanic*, they were very orderly in getting the boats ready to be loaded. At 12:25 A.M., nearly an hour after the collision, Captain Smith gave the order to start loading the lifeboats with women and children.

First Officer Murdoch was in charge of the boats on the ship's port, or left side, while Second Officer Charles Lightoller was responsible for the boats on the starboard, or right, side. When Lightoller made the first call for women and children to get into lifeboat No. 6, some passengers were still not convinced of the danger. They felt certain that rescue ships would arrive long before the *Titanic* went under, if it ever went under at all. John Jacob

Astor, the richest man on the ship, was not ready to depend on a wooden lifeboat for his survival.

"We are safer here than in that little boat," he said to those around him.[9]

The ship's small orchestra had set up their instruments on the boat deck and were playing music. Their presence helped add a sense of calm to what was happening on the deck.

A few of the women refused to get into a boat without their husbands. When no more women came forward, a few couples and a few other men were allowed to get in. At 12:45 A.M., boat No. 7 on the ship's port side became the first boat to be lowered into the water. It was large enough to carry sixty-five people. But because of confusion, and many passengers' reluctance to leave the *Titanic*, the boat was lowered with only twenty-eight people in it.

Up on the bridge, Fourth Officer Joseph Boxhall ordered quartermaster George Rowe to begin firing distress rockets. Rowe fired the first rocket, which scattered twelve brilliant flares into the sky. Rowe fired a new rocket every five minutes so that any passing ships could spot the *Titanic*.

At about the same time, Boxhall observed the lights of a ship passing within five or six miles of the *Titanic*. He used a Morse code lamp to send flashes of a distress code to the other ship. But the ship slowly turned and vanished over the horizon. More than an hour after the collision there was no rescue in sight.

The *Carpathia* was fifty-eight miles away from the *Titanic* when it received the ship's distress call. It immediately headed full-steam to the legendary liner's rescue.

Wireless operators John Phillips and Harold Bride continued to send out calls for assistance. A number of ships had responded, but they were all too far away to help the *Titanic*. The closest ship to respond was the *Carpathia*. Its wireless operator tapped out a message that it was fifty-eight miles away, and heading full steam to the *Titanic*'s rescue.

But the *Carpathia* would not arrive in time. The *Titanic*'s bow was already dipping far into the water. The tilt of the decks was growing steeper. Those who had doubts earlier could now see that the mighty ship was really sinking. Passengers began to crowd around the lifeboats. They started loading into the lifeboats in larger numbers.

Many of the third-class passengers were kept below decks. This was done to keep the boat decks from getting too crowded. This meant that only first- and second-class passengers were getting into the lifeboats. Third-class passengers were not. As the ship's decks tilted further, the *Titanic*'s doom became clear to everyone. Panic was brewing below decks.

Crewmen continued to load the boats with mostly women and children. Molly Brown was walking away from the deck area when she was grabbed and dropped into boat No. 6.

Wealthy businessman Isidor Straus and his wife chose to go down with the ship. They allowed others to board the lifeboats instead.

Wealthy businessman Isidor Straus decided that he would stay with the big ship and leave space for others on the lifeboats. Crewmen and others on deck encouraged his wife to get into one of the boats.

"We have been living together for many years," she told her husband. "Where you go, I go."[10]

The wife of French novelist Jacques Futrelle also would not get into a lifeboat.

"For God's sake, go!" her husband told her. "It's your last chance! Go!" As she continued to protest, an officer decided the matter by forcing her into a lifeboat.[11]

Twelve-year-old Ruth Becker watched her younger brother and sister get loaded into boat No. 11. The crew suddenly began to lower the boat.

"Oh, let me go with my children!" Ruth's mother screamed, and jumped into the boat with them. Ruth was left standing on the deck.[12]

Her mother called back to Ruth to get into another lifeboat. Ruth went down the deck to the next lifeboat. She asked the officer if she could get in. The officer picked her up and put her in a boat. It was so full that she had to stand up. As the crowded boat neared the water, another boat was lowered nearly on top of them. A man in Ruth's boat pulled out a knife and cut their boat free from the ropes. Ruth's boat pushed away from the side of the ship just seconds before the other boat would have landed on top of them.

By 1:30 A.M., panic was spreading. The *Titanic*'s bow was submerged. The decks continued to slant toward the water. Many people were still aboard and only a few lifeboats were left. The *Titanic*'s time was running out.

CHAPTER 4

Swallowed by the Sea

Disorder grew among the *Titanic*'s passengers. They became more anxious to get into the lifeboats. Fifth Officer Harold Lowe drew his revolver. He fired three warning shots along the outside of the ship. He wanted to keep passengers from crowding against the remaining boats.

By 1:50 A.M., the ship's sixteen wooden lifeboats were away. Only the four collapsible boats were left. Crewmen began loading collapsible boat D. Second Officer Lightoller ordered them to lock arms and form a circle around the boat. Only women and children were allowed to pass through and climb aboard.

At another part of the ship, the wealthy American industrialist Benjamin Guggenheim and his aide Victor Giglio emerged from their cabins. They had taken off their sweaters and lifejackets and changed into tuxedos and ties.

Passengers on the lifeboats could only watch helplessly as the *Titanic* sank beneath the icy waves.

"We've dressed in our best and are prepared to go down like gentlemen," Guggenheim said.[1]

At about 2 A.M., Captain Smith told the wireless operators they were relieved of duty. But after the captain left, Phillips and Bride kept working for several more minutes. Captain Smith relieved every crewmember he saw on his way back to the bridge. Standing on the *Titanic*'s bridge, he waited for its plunge into the sea.

Water flooded up through the lower decks. Passengers hurried away from the rising water. The small orchestra on the boat deck played their last song, "Nearer, My God, to Thee." Then they broke up to await their fates.

The attempt to launch collapsible boat B ended when

the *Titanic*'s sinking bow plunged Second Officer Lightoller and others into the water. Swimming in the icy water, they tried to climb onto the overturned boat.

The ship's stern tilted into the air, slowly rising higher above the water. Boilers within the ship exploded, killing crewmen and passengers who were still below. As the ship sank deeper into the water, waves passed by, sweeping people out to sea.

More than 1,500 people were still aboard, and no rescue ships were in sight. But the *Titanic*'s moments were numbered. The stern rose higher and higher above the sea as water flooded the bow. From her lifeboat, Ruth Becker watched the *Titanic*'s final moments.

"I could look back and see this ship, and the decks were just lined with people looking over," she later said. "Finally, as the *Titanic* sank faster, the lights died out. You could just see the stern remaining in an upright position for a couple of minutes. Then . . . it disappeared."[2]

Another passenger, August Wennerstrom, floated a safe distance away. He watched the scene from his collapsible boat.

"It was horrible," he said, "but at the same time, in a way that I am unable to explain, wonderfully dramatic."[3]

Helen Candee, in another lifeboat, also witnessed the end of the *Titanic*.

"At the last," she said, "the end of the world . . . she went down with an awful grating."[4]

The massive ocean liner had vanished into the sea. Hundreds of people were left floating in the freezing water. A handful of men climbed onto collapsible boat B. A few others were hauled out of the water by people in lifeboats. But most were just left in the water.

Molly Brown insisted that her lifeboat, No. 6, row toward the surviving swimmers. She wanted to rescue as many people as possible before they froze. But crewman Robert Hitchens and passenger Arthur Peuchen were arguing over who was in command of the lifeboat. Hitchens would not listen to Molly's pleas. Frederick Fleet, the lookout who had originally spotted the iceberg, was the only other man on board to work the oars. Molly showed the other women how to row. But many of them were afraid they would all be dumped into the water if they tried to rescue other people. As arguments continued among Brown, Hitchens, and Peuchen, the women worked the oars to keep warm. But no rescues were made.[5]

The cries of people in the water gradually quieted, then stopped. They had survived the actual sinking but slowly froze to death in the water. Of the hundreds who had jumped into the water when the ship sank, only twelve survived.

It was nearly two hours before a ship, the *Carpathia*, arrived to pull the survivors aboard to safety. The *Carpathia* shot flares into the sky to alert other ships that the survivors had been found. Many of the lifeboats were close to sinking by the time the *Carpathia* got to them.

Second Officer Lightoller and wireless operator Harold Bride were among the thirty men who spent the night clinging to the top of collapsible boat B. A few of the men had frozen and quietly slid into the water during the night. Their boat was so low in the water that Lightoller was afraid the *Carpathia* would not see them. He pulled out his pocket whistle and blew on it several times. The ship eventually came to rescue them. Officer Lightoller was the last *Titanic* survivor to climb aboard the *Carpathia.*[6]

When the search for survivors ended at about 8 A.M., the *Carpathia*'s crew had pulled only 705 *Titanic* crew members and passengers from the Atlantic. The rest, 1,503 people, were dead. Wireless reports from the *Carpathia* sent the news back to England and ahead to New York, where the ship would arrive in three days.

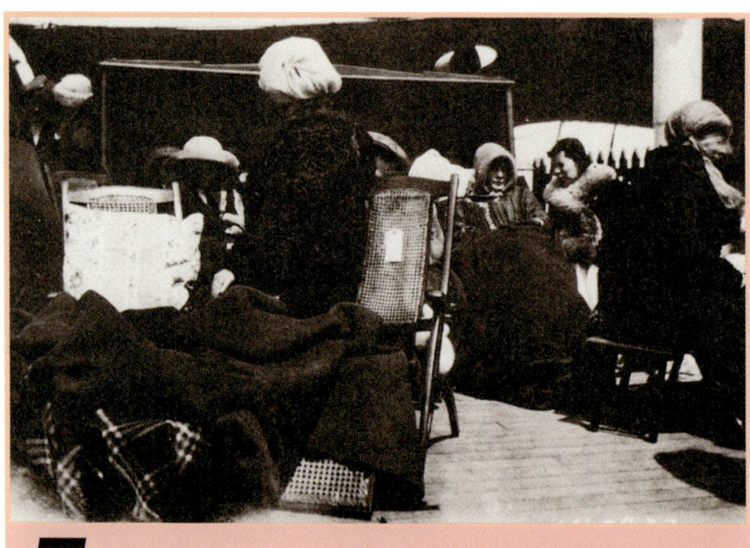

***Titanic* survivors huddle together on the deck of the *Carpathia*.**

Newspapers around the world gave banner headlines to the tragic story.

On the evening of April 18, 1912, the *Carpathia* arrived in New York harbor, carrying the *Titanic*'s survivors. Even though it was the middle of a rainstorm, thirty thousand people were waiting along the docks.

The White Star Line hired a ship from Nova Scotia to search for bodies at the site of the sinking, an area about 500 miles southeast of Newfoundland. After two weeks, the crew had pulled 328 bodies from the water. About half of the bodies were identified and claimed by loved ones for burial. Some were so badly decomposed, or decayed, that they could not be identified. They were buried at sea after a service by a clergyman on the ship. The remaining 150 unclaimed bodies were buried in three cemeteries in Halifax, Nova Scotia.

The survivors went on with their lives, but none would ever forget this dramatic disaster. They were often asked to retell the stories of their experiences during the sinking. Molly Brown was interviewed by many newspaper reporters after arriving in New York. Responding to the question of how she survived the disaster, Brown told one reporter she was unsinkable. This is how she became known as "the unsinkable Mrs. Brown."

Immediately after the tragedy, a series of investigations was begun. By learning exactly what went wrong with the *Titanic*, it was hoped that such a disaster at sea would never happen again.

Investigations by both the United States Senate and

"Unsinkable" Molly Brown emerged as a true hero in the aftermath of the *Titanic* disaster, due to her determination to save as many lives as possible.

the British Board of Trade agreed that the construction of the hull compartments was flawed. The hull compartments should not have allowed water to spill upward into the higher decks.

The British investigation was not very critical of Captain Smith. But the American investigators felt that Captain Smith had been careless. They felt he should have slowed or stopped the ship after receiving the repeated ice warnings. In fact, Captain Smith had increased the ship to almost full speed after the warnings.

Also, no special lookout had been ordered when the *Titanic* entered the area where icebergs had been reported. There was not even a pair of binoculars in the crow's nest.

The two investigations also found fault with Captain Stanley Lord of the ocean liner *Californian.* The *Californian* may have been the ship that Fourth Officer Boxhall saw passing by about an hour after the collision. Investigators found that crewmen aboard the *Californian* had seen all eight of the *Titanic*'s distress rockets, and reported them to their captain. But Captain Lord did nothing. He did not even order anyone to turn on the wireless machine to listen for a distress call.

During the hours after the collision, the *Californian* was the only ship that passed near the *Titanic.* If Captain Lord and his crew had responded to the *Titanic*'s rockets, most of those aboard the *Titanic* would likely have been saved.[7]

Both investigations found the White Star Line unprepared for an emergency on the *Titanic.* The company should have had more than two times the number of lifeboats available on the ship. Also, the crew was never required to conduct a lifeboat drill during the trip. The crew's lack of practice added to the confusion as people were boarding the lifeboats.

The investigations into the *Titanic*'s sinking resulted in a number of new laws. Every ship at sea now had to have a radio operator on duty at all times. This was done to keep track of navigation warnings. In addition, the United States created the International Ice Patrol. This patrol keeps a constant count of icebergs and reports their positions to nearby ships. Probably the most important new law required all ships to carry enough lifeboats for all crew members and passengers on board.[8]

The investigations were over by the middle of 1912. But nothing would ever end the public's interest in the *Titanic.*

In this photo from 1991, the bow of the *Titanic* emerges hauntingly out of the darkness. It lies more than 12,500 feet below the surface of the northern Atlantic Ocean.

CHAPTER 5

A Legendary Tragedy

The *Titanic*'s sinking is a legendary disaster for many reasons. There are qualities about it that touch on all our human hopes and fears.

This tragedy is full of touching stories. The band played on the deck as the ship sank. Guggenheim and his aide dressed in tuxedos to "go down like gentlemen." Molly Brown insisted that her lifeboat go back to pull out survivors. The ship's officers and crew members performed many heroic deeds. Many passengers displayed great courage.

There are also many "what ifs" that might have changed the fate of the *Titanic*. What if the lookouts had been using binoculars? What if Captain Smith had not increased the ship's speed? What if the officer on the bridge had not reversed the engines after the iceberg was sighted?

There are many mysteries as well. Why did the ship seen in the distance never come to the *Titanic*'s rescue?

Why did so many ships fail to respond to its distress signals? Was Captain Smith made aware of all the iceberg warnings before he gave the order to increase speed?

For more than seventy years, the greatest mystery was the actual location of the sunken ship. In 1985, that mystery was solved.

Shortly after midnight on September 1, 1985, Dr. Robert Ballard and his crew on the research ship *Knorr* discovered the wreckage of the *Titanic*. A year later, Ballard and a team of scientists explored the wreckage

This section of the *Titanic*'s hull was recovered in 1998. It is the largest fragment of the legendary ship to have reached the surface since the ship sank almost a century ago.

site. They used the submersible vehicle *Alvin*. A submersible vehicle can go underwater for deep-sea research.

Ballard's explorations showed that the massive ship had snapped in half before sinking more than 12,000 feet to the bottom of the Atlantic Ocean. The bow and stern sections of the ship sat on the ocean floor nearly 2,000 feet apart. Thousands of pieces of debris were littered in between.[1]

Millions of people around the world have seen the haunting photographs and videotapes of the sunken ship

This docking bridge telegraph is one of the items taken from the wreckage of the *Titanic*.

taken by Ballard's team. A few items were taken to be displayed in museums, but the ship remains on the bottom of the ocean. No human remains were found during Ballard's explorations.

The story of the *Titanic* teaches an important lesson. It shows that no human activity can be free from error. Even our greatest achievements are not safe from the possibility of disaster.

Other Nautical Disasters

February 24, 1852—South Africa—HMS *Birkenhead* sinks off the coast of South Africa. Of the 638 people aboard, only 193 survive. The tradition of "women and children first" begins here.
July 24, 1915—Chicago, Illinois—The passenger ship *Eastland* overturns on the Chicago River while preparing to depart for a Lake Michigan cruise. The disaster claims over 800 lives.
December 6, 1917—Halifax, Nova Scotia—The munitions ship, the *Mont Blanc*, collides with the *Imo*, a Belgian relief ship. Explosives carried aboard the *Mont Blanc* are set off as a result, incinerating the ship and blowing its anchor miles away. Shards of glass and other debris injure many in the biggest man-made explosion before the atomic bomb. 1,963 people are killed and approximately 9,000 are injured.
July 25, 1956—United States—The *Andrea Doria* is struck by the Swedish-American liner *Stockholm*, sixty miles off the coast of Nantucket. 52 passengers die; 1,662 survive.
April 10, 1963—United States—U.S. submarine *Thresher* sinks off the coast of New England due to equipment failure caused by a leak in the engine room. 129 crew members die with no survivors.
August 12, 2000—Russia—Russian nuclear submarine *Kursk* sinks in the Barents Sea possibly due to the torpedo compartments flooding after firing. 118 die; none survive.

Chapter Notes

Chapter 1. Unsinkable

1. Charles Pellegrino, *Her Name, Titanic* (New York: McGraw Hill Publishing Company, 1988), p. 101.

2. John P. Eaton and Charles A. Haas, *Titanic: Triumph and Tragedy* (New York: W.W. Norton & Company, 1994), p. 137.

Chapter 2. The Biggest and Finest

1. John P. Eaton and Charles A. Haas, *Titanic: Triumph and Tragedy* (New York: W.W. Norton & Company, 1994), pp. 20–31.

2. Robert D. Ballard, *Exploring the Titanic* (Toronto, Ontario: Madison Publishing Inc., 1988), p. 10.

3. Beverly McMillan and Stanley Lehrer, *Titanic: Fortune and Fate* (New York: Simon and Schuster, 1998), p. 16.

4. Walter Lord, *A Night to Remember* (New York: Bantam Books, 1955), p. 26.

5. Ballard, p. 11.

6. McMillan and Lehrer, p. 27.

7. Eaton and Haas, pp. 114–115.

8. Ibid., p. 137.

Chapter 3. The Impossible Happens

1. John P. Eaton and Charles A. Haas, *Titanic: Triumph and Tragedy* (New York: W.W. Norton & Company, 1994), p. 137.

2. Robert D. Ballard, *Exploring the Titanic* (Toronto, Ontario: Madison Publishing Inc., 1988), p. 20.

3. Charles Pellegrino, *Her Name, Titanic* (New York: McGraw Hill Publishing Company, 1988), p. 21.

4. Walter Lord, *A Night to Remember* (New York: Bantam Books, 1955), p. 8.

5. Eaton and Haas, p. 143.

6. Wyn Craig Wade, *The Titanic: End of a Dream* (New York: Rawson, Wade Publishers, Inc., 1979), p. 31.

7. Eaton and Haas, p. 145.

8. Ballard, p. 23.

9. Lord, p. 43.

10. Pellegrino, p. 172.

11. Eaton and Haas, p. 152.

12. Beverly McMillan and Stanley Lehrer, *Titanic: Fortune and Fate* (New York: Simon and Schuster, 1998), p. 82.

Chapter 4. Swallowed by the Sea

1. Beverly McMillan and Stanley Lehrer, *Titanic: Fortune and Fate* (New York: Simon and Schuster, 1998), p. 41.

2. Robert D. Ballard, *Exploring the Titanic* (Toronto, Ontario: Madison Publishing Inc., 1988), p. 29.

3. Wyn Craig Wade, *The Titanic: End of a Dream* (New York: Rawson, Wade Publishers, Inc., 1979), pp. 213–214.

4. Ibid., p. 214.

5. Walter Lord, *A Night to Remember* (New York: Bantam Books, 1955), pp. 128–129.

6. John P. Eaton and Charles A. Haas, *Titanic: Triumph and Tragedy* (New York: W.W. Norton & Company, 1994), p. 179.

7. Wade, pp. 237–241.

8. Eaton and Haas, pp. 259–275.

Chapter 5. A Legendary Tragedy

1. Robert D. Ballard, *Exploring the Titanic* (Toronto, Ontario: Madison Publishing Inc., 1988), pp. 38–60.

Glossary

bow—The front end of a ship.

bridge—An elevated room or structure toward the front of the ship where crew members have a clear view ahead, and from which the ship is navigated.

CQD—A Morse code signal used in the early days of wireless communication. It meant "Come, Quick, Danger."

crow's nest—A lookout platform high on a ship's mast.

dry dock—A dock out of the water that is used for the construction and repair of ships.

hull—The frame or body of a ship.

lifeboat—A boat carried aboard a larger ship for use in emergencies.

maiden voyage—The first voyage of a new ship.

Morse code—A code invented by Samuel Morse, made up of a series of dots and dashes to represent letters of the alphabet. The messages could be sent by tapping out sounds on a radio or by flashing a Morse lamp.

Morse lamp—A lamp used to flash signals in Morse code.

port—The left side of a ship, as seen when facing forward.

starboard—The right side of a ship, as seen when facing forward.

stern—The rear end of a ship.

steward—A ship's crew member who attends to the needs of passengers.

wireless—An early form of radio communication that carried electronic code bleeps, but not voice communication.

Further Reading

Adams, Simon. *Titanic.* New York: D.K. Publishing, 1999.

Ballard, Robert D. *Exploring the Titanic.* Toronto, Ontario: Madison Publishing Inc., 1988.

Conklin, Thomas. *The Titanic Sinks!* New York: Random House, 1997.

Stacey, Tom. *The Titanic.* San Diego: Lucent Books, 1989.

Tanaka, Shelly. *On Board the Titanic.* New York: Hyperion Books, 1998.

Internet Addresses

Hind, Philip. *Encyclopedia Titanica.* <http://www.encyclopedia-titanica.org/> (September 25, 2000).

RMS Titanic, Inc. Online. <http://www.titanic-online.com/> (September 25, 2000).

Titanic Information Site. <http://www.skarr.com/titanic/> (September 25, 2000).

Titanic, Olympic & Britannic Homepage. <http://www.titanic.cc/> (September 25, 2000).

The Titanic Resource. <http://www.titanicresource.8m.com/titanic.htm> (September 25, 2000).

A Tribute to the RMS Titanic. <http://www.fireflyproductions.com/titanic/> (September 25, 2000).

Index